Successful
Allotments

Gardening **organically**

One of the great joys of gardening is to experience the variety of life that a healthy garden contains. A garden managed using organic methods will have far more interest in it than a garden where insecticides and chemicals are used. An organic garden is a more balanced environment, where 'good' creatures such as ladybirds and beetles keep the 'bad' pests and diseases under control.

Organically grown plants also tend to be healthier and stronger than plants that rely on large doses of artificial fertiliser. In healthy soil they grow strong roots and can better withstand attack by pests and diseases. Soil can be kept in top condition by recycling garden waste to make nutritious compost. Growing the right combination of plants in the right place at the right time – by rotating where you plant your veg for example, or choosing shrubs to suit the growing conditions that your garden can offer – can deliver impressive disease-free results.

These are the basic principles of organic growing – use the natural resources you already have to create a balanced and vibrant garden. It's sustainable, cheaper than buying chemicals, easier than you think and great fun. Enjoy your organic gardening.

Allotments have huge value – as open space, as wildlife havens, as places to unwind and find peace, as well as their more obvious use in the production of fresh, free, local food. Walk through the gates of your local allotment site and you will be entering another world…

Urban allotments were first created in the 19th century, for the landless working classes to grow their own food. Reaching a peak of 1.5 million sites during the second world war, numbers declined dramatically to a low of 200,000 sites as interest waned and sites were closed.

Fortunately, allotments have undergone something of a revolution. No longer the sole province of ageing men, they are moving forward into the 21st century rejuvenated by a whole new community of plot holders from all walks of life – an exciting mix of age, race, culture and gender. And an increasing number are managed organically.

Contents

1

Choosing a site

Choosing an allotment site

An allotment is a plot of land, approximately 25sq m in size, that can be rented for growing food. Allotments are usually found grouped together on an allotment site – which may have dozens, or even hundreds, of plots.

The majority of allotment sites are owned by Local Authorities. Some are managed directly by the Local Authority, while others have a committee, made up of allotment holders, who manage the site.

The benefit of a Local Authority site, is that the majority are 'statutory' sites, which cannot easily be sold off for development. Some Local Authority sites are 'temporary' and will eventually be reclaimed by the Local Authority for other uses, such as a cemetery.

Around 8% of sites are privately owned – the owner of the land usually renting the land to the allotment association/ group. The number of these sites is declining as the price of land goes up, but new ones are also being set up. Allotment sites can be tucked away, so you may not even realise they are there

Finding an allotment

- The internet – many allotment societies and groups have their own websites
- In the library – they may hold lists
- Ask locally
- Ring your local council
- Try the parish council

Allotment sites vary in the facilities they offer, the rules and regulations they enforce, the rent charged and their attitude to children, women, organics and so on. If you have a choice of sites, check them all before making a decision. Talk to plot holders to get a 'feel' of the place.

Location - Close to home, ideally within walking distance, is the most practical, and the most likely to retain your enthusiasm.

Check site rules and regulations – If you want to plant fruit trees, keep hens, paint your shed, use a plastic mulch or grow flowers you may not be able to on some sites! If you fancy more of a 'leisure garden', or at least a patch of lawn for the kids to play on, check that this is allowed.

Do you hate bonfires? Some sites don't allow them; others restrict burning to certain days.

The cost - The average annual rent for an allotment plot is £25 – though rents can be as little as 50p or as much as £100. This usually includes the cost of water, but may not. There may be reductions for pensioners etc.

Organic plots - If you want to grow organically, ask if there is a specific 'organic area'. Don't be put off if the answer is no. You can still run a successful organic plot, and, as you succeed, others may follow. There are few all organic sites.

Good society - Some allotment sites have a very active community with a trading shed, a meeting place or mentors offering to help newcomers for example. Some will welcome families with children, and there may even, occasionally, be toilets on site.

Vandalism - By their very nature, allotments are at risk from vandalism – though lots of people never have any problems.

Tips for choosing your plot

- Find a site close to home, preferably within walking distance

- Check out site rules and regulations before you choose

- If you have children, find out if families are welcome

- Be sure there is an adequate water supply for the plot; use of a hose is rarely allowed

- Take on a recently vacated plot if possible

- Take on a half sized plot to start with if a larger plot looks too demanding

- Ask if there is an organic area on the site

- If it is not a statutory site, ask how secure the tenancy is

- Ask about vandalism and site security

- Is there somewhere to park, and access for delivery of manure and leaves?

2

Creating your ideal allotment

Planning your plot

If you take over a well cared for plot, you may decide to work with the current layout, only making changes when you have gained some experience. Even a well managed plot may not be exactly right for you – if you have children perhaps, or want to spend less time there than your predecessor.

On the other hand you may start with a run down, weedy plot. This gives you the opportunity to start from scratch with your own plans.

Decide what you want on your plot

Measure up the plot and draw a large plan. Mark on it existing 'features', such as weedy areas, crops, shed, water points, paths, access road etc.

Decide what you want from your allotment. Is it maximum food production, or would you like flowers and a lawn too? Does it need to be child-friendly? Can you give it lots of time from the start, or will you develop it slowly? Add features to the plan as you make your decisions.

Shed and **fencing**

A shed is useful for storage, and sheltering from the weather. Second hand sheds may be available if there isn't one there already. Guttering on the shed will channel rainwater from the roof into a waterbutt (or two).

Some allotments, particularly where there is livestock on site, are fenced individually. This also keeps other people's dogs and children off the plot, and yours in!

You may inherit a shed with your plot; make sure you can catch rainwater from the roof.

Space for manure, autumn leaves and compost

You may want a delivery of animal manure, autumn leaves or green waste compost to your plot. Allow space near the road for a lorry or tractor to drop a load. Store manure under a sheet of plastic and leaves in a simple wire netting cage. Aim for at least 2 cages, each 1m square.

Plan for at least two compost heaps/ bins. Allow 1m square for each, plus space around for working. You may prefer a permanent site for making compost, or choose to have bins scattered around the plot. You can make cheap compost bins from scrap wood and other recycled materials.

Relax and play areas

Allotmenting shouldn't be all about hard work. Plan in somewhere to sit and relax and enjoy the fresh air, or a play area for the children.

Make space for creating compost – it is the 'free' fertiliser that will keep your plot blooming.

Tips for **child-friendly** allotments

- Divide the plot up into beds with clearly defined paths, so kids know where to walk and not to walk

- Allocate an area for children to grow what they want

- Buy them proper children's gardening tools, not play tools

- Involve children in harvesting – much more immediately rewarding than sowing seeds

- Make a grassy area for playing

- Make sure there is safe space undercover, and a tasteful bucket as an emergency loo

- Ask them to help choose what you grow

- Plant lots of flowers

- Grow halloween pumpkins

- Have competitions for the tallest flower, the heaviest potato or the biggest pumpkin

Fruit trees and bushes

Black and redcurrants and gooseberries can be grown as bushes; redcurrants and gooseberries can also be trained against a fence. Blackberries and hybrid berries and grapes need to be trained against a fence or wires. Apples, pears and plums can also be grown as trained forms or as trees.

Raspberries are grown in rows and strawberries are often given their own bed, which needs to be moved every three or four years.

Rhubarb, which is really a vegetable, is a traditional easy to grow allotment crop.

As fruit plants will be in the ground for many years, allocate them a permanent, sunny spot where they will not shade other crops.

For more information on choosing and growing fruit, see *Grow Fruit* in the *Green Essentials* series .

Flowers and herbs

You may want to grow flowers for
cutting or to brighten up the plot,
or to feed beneficial insects to
promote natural pest control – or all
three of course. They can be grown
in the vegetable beds, or given
separate areas.

Annual herbs are usually included
in the vegetable beds. You may
have a separate area for perennial
herbs such as rosemary, marjoram
and thyme.

*Attract beneficial
insects with flowers –
they can help to
protect your crops.*

A pond and other wildlife features

Ponds are great for wildlife, particularly for frogs and toads that love to eat slugs, and can provide hours of fun pond gazing and dipping. A pond needs to be in an open sunny spot, but check with the site rules before you start to dig.

There are loads of other creatures that eat pests – from hedgehogs to black beetles, spiders and centipedes. They play a vital part in keeping pests down on the plot. All need places to rest up safe from their predators, and places to breed. They will enjoy soil-covering mulches, heaps of logs and areas of undisturbed grass and vegetation. See *Attract Wildlife* in the *Green Essentials* series for further information.

Paths

A good network of paths will help you to avoid walking on growing areas. A path for a wheel barrow should be at least the width of your barrow, with extra width for turning space at corners. Narrower paths between the wider ones are fine if you are nimble footed. Paths should follow the most direct route if possible.

Vegetables

Asparagus, globe artichokes, sea kale and rhubarb are perennial vegetables which need their own permanent growing area. The largest area on an allotment is usually given over to growing annual vegetables. See page 35 for more about growing vegetables.

Livestock

Some allotment sites allow no livestock, while others may allow poultry, rabbits or even goats. You will need to take separate advice on keeping animals on an allotment.

An old compost bin makes a good cover for blanching rhubarb in early spring. Although technically a vegetable, rhubarb is usually thought of as a fruit.

Tips for planning your allotment

- Make a plan of your new plot, recording everything that is on it and where the sunny and shady spots will be

- Assess the condition and type of soil you have – e.g sandy and light or clayey and heavy to dig

- Decide on what you want on your plot

- Play with new layouts, including all your requirements, with sticky notes until you get it right

- List the fruit and vegetables you want to grow

- Plan in wildlife features to help with pest control

- Check rules and regulations before you start

- Remember to leave sufficient space for compost, manure and leaf heaps

3

Getting started

Health and **safety** issues

- Check your tetanus injections are up to date

- Wear sturdy footwear when digging/forking

- Wear steel toe-capped boots when using powered machinery

- Keep all sharp tools stored safely

- Keep cuts covered

- Wash your hands before eating

- Take care of your back. Do some warm up exercises before you start work, and take regular breaks, especially when digging

- Use a spade, fork and hoe that suit your size and strength

When to start

In the past, allotments traditionally changed hands on 29th September – Michaelmas Day, the set day for paying agricultural rents. This is a good time to take over a plot. It gives you time to prepare for the following year, often in reasonable weather. Many allotment sites use the calendar year, or start at other times – but it's worth contacting them at any time of year to see if they have vacancies, or a waiting list.

The key to long-term success with an allotment is to be realistic about how much you can tackle. Take things slowly, planning to do less than the maximum. It may take several years to get things as you would like them. The whole point about allotmenting is that it should be recreational, fun even, not a chore – and it doesn't have to be a competition with your neighbours!

Tools and **equipment**

If you don't already have a collection of gardening tools, take time to choose what you need for the allotment. Always handle a tool before purchase so you know you are comfortable with it. Handle length is crucial for spades, forks, hoes and rakes. Look out for longer or shorter handles if necessary.

If you are tall, buy a rake or hoe head on its own, then fit a longer handle. Weight is also important - remember that a spade will be loaded with soil in use, so don't buy one that feels heavy when you pick it up empty. A border spade or fork, which has a smaller head, is often a good choice. You will be able to keep working longer if each full spade is not an effort. If possible try out other people's tools on the ground first. When buying tools for children, make sure that they are designed for proper use, not just as toys.

Second hand tools are often available through ads in the papers or at car boot sales. They will generally work just as well as new ones, at a fraction of the price.

As many allotment plots are infected with soil borne pests and diseases, it can pay to have separate allotment tools to avoid transferring diseases to your garden soil.

You may have to water with a can, so look carefully at where your water supply is sited.

A selection of plastic buckets will be useful for collecting weeds and distributing compost.

Hoes come in various shapes and sizes for different uses such as weed control, forming a 'drill' to sow seeds into and earthing up potatoes, so you may end up with several. A wide blade is useful for clearing a large area; a narrow blade better for hoeing between plants. Keep the edge sharp for efficient use.

Paths should be wide enough to allow for wheelbarrow access and turning.

Useful **allotment tools** and equipment

- Spade, garden fork, hoe and trowel

- Mattock for clearing a weedy plot

- Wheelbarrow

- Large buckets - for collecting weeds in

- Rake - one with a wider head (60cm) is most practical

- Sharp penknife

- Petrol or hand mower, petrol strimmer or scythe to maintain grassy areas

- Watering cans

- A couple of comfy chairs

- Sticks, string and plant labels

- Long tape measure

- Bamboo canes - for climbing beans

- Black plastic sheeting

- Pencil and notebook

Clearing an overgrown plot

Clearing **without weedkillers**

If you take on an overgrown plot don't despair; just take it slowly. Clear and plant manageable sections. Mow or mulch the rest to keep it under control.

Your first action must be to walk the plot, removing any debris. It is amazing what people dump on allotments. Wear thick gloves. You might even find some edible vegetables if you are lucky.

Look at the various ways of clearing weeds described below and choose which suits you. You might, for example, decide to clear an area by hand for planting up this year, grow potatoes directly into another area, mulch some and mow the rest for the first year.

Clearing **by hand**

Cut down tall growth with a scythe or mower. Then, using a mattock, or sharp spade, roughly break up the ground. Break it down further with a fork and remove all weeds and roots. Go over the ground several times, over a period of weeks, as you are unlikely to get all the weed roots the first time.

Digging stimulates weed seeds to grow, so it helps if your first crops are fast growing transplants – pumpkins, brussels sprouts, courgettes, cabbages or corn for example – that can be mulched or hoed to keep them weed free. Avoid direct sown crops such as carrots or parsnips in the first year.

Sow green manures (alfalfa, clover, mustard and rye are popular) on ground that you won't be otherwise sowing or planting up for a few weeks. See page 58 for more details.

Perennial weed roots you might encounter

Bindweed – spreads by white, creeping underground stems that break easily – very hard to eliminate.

Couchgrass – tough, shallow growing, underground rhizomes that look like roots. Easily pulled out of soil that has been dug over.

Docks – plants produce a thick tap root. Pull whole plant out of ground.

A thick layer of mulch will help to control weeds; but you will have to work to control bindweed (top).

'Nasty weed' compost heap

Instead of burning perennial weeds, wasting the plant foods they contain, make them into their own compost heap, covered with black plastic. After a year or two, when the roots are no longer visible, the compost is safe to use.

Mulching

A light excluding mulch, such as black plastic sheet or cardboard (opened out boxes, weighted down with straw) will stop weeds growing, and gradually kill them. Even a few months of cover will make the soil much easier to dig over; a year or so will get rid of almost all weeds.

If you are keen to get growing, try planting a crop such as pumpkins or broccoli through holes cut in the mulch.

Growing **potatoes**

Potatoes can be planted into weedy ground as a 'clearing' crop. Plant them in trenches dug in the soil about 1m apart. Earth the plants up regularly as they grow, then keep hand weeding. The crop may not be huge but the ground will be much clearer by the time you have dug the potatoes.

Alternatively, try a crop of 'no dig' potatoes, grown under a straw mulch (see *Grow Vegetables* in the *Green Essentials* series).

Rotavating

A powered cultivator may seem an attractive option for clearing a weedy plot – but it has its disadvantages. Cultivating a weedy plot can be strenuous work; you may like to hire an operator with the machine. On some sites, other plot holders may offer a rotavating service.

A powered cultivator chops weed roots up into small pieces, most of which will grow again. Digging these out by hand is a tedious job so, realistically, the ground needs to be rotavated again once green weed shoots begin to appear. A third go may be necessary.

Cutting down

If the ground is level, simply mow the weeds now and again. This can turn an area into a rough 'lawn'.

A crop of pumpkins can be grown while clearing ground. When the soil is warm, cut down vegetation and cover area with cardboard. Plant into prepared planting holes, surrounding each plant with a square of black plastic (bin liners will do).

Tips for clearing a weedy plot

- Invite friends around to help – offer them a picnic lunch

- Divide the task up into manageable chunks

- Only clear as much as you will be able to keep clear

- Cover weeds with a plastic mulch to start killing them off

- Mow or strim to stop weeds from spreading

- Cut off flower heads of perennial weeds to prevent them seeding

- Don't plant raspberry canes, or put edging around beds until the ground is really free of perennial weeds. Otherwise you will never get rid of them

- Don't burn off the weeds – it will harm wildlife and annoy neighbours

- Don't scrape off the weedy layer – this is where the best topsoil will be

- Keep some large sheets of black plastic to hand to cover cleared areas that you don't have time to plant up immediately

Vegetable growing – rows or beds

Traditionally an allotment plot is divided up into 4 areas for growing vegetables to allow for a crop rotation (see page 43). Vegetables are grown in long rows across each section.

Nowadays many people are choosing to grow in narrow (1.25m wide) beds, divided by access paths. Digging, weeding, planting and so on is done from the paths, so the beds can be very intensively planted, giving high returns – which make up for the area of ground given over to paths.

Both ways work well – it's really down to personal preference. Beds are great when gardening with children as they clearly define the boundary between path and crop.

Vegetables grown in traditional rows.

Making a bed

A bed is made simply by marking out a rectangle, 1.25m wide x the length you choose. Mark each corner with a stout stick, and the perimeter of the bed with a length of string.

Wooden edges around beds look smart, but are not vital. Edging is good for keeping path mulches off the soil, but can also act as a hideaway for slugs. Clear all perennial weeds before installing permanent edging.

Making **paths**

Make paths as maintenance free as possible to save time later. Don't make anything permanent until the ground is clear of perennial weeds; otherwise paths can just be a continual source of weed problems.

Path **surfaces**

Bare earth - The simplest. Muddy in wet weather. Regular hoeing needed.

Grass – Looks nice, but can be muddy over winter. Regular mowing, and cutting the edges, is essential to prevent grass invading the growing areas.

Loose mulches – Wood chip, shredded prunings, autumn leaves, straw, hay. Layer at least 5-10cm thick. Can remove a 5-10cm layer of topsoil first to reduce weeds growing through. Nice to look at and walk or kneel on. Will need to be topped up as mulch decays. Mulches will tend to stray into growing areas unless paths (or beds) have a containing edging.

Plastic mulches – Should be permeable so water doesn't collect and covered with a loose mulch. Stops weeds growing from below, but can be slippy.

Paving slabs – More pricey, but weed free and weather proof.

Tips for getting started

- Don't try and prepare the whole plot at once

- Mulch around your first crops to minimise weeds

- Grow potatoes to help clear the soil of weeds

- Grow vegetables in narrow beds with dividing paths for easy access

- Plant green manure crops on unused parts of your plot to keep the soil healthy and keep weeds at bay

4

What can I grow on my allotment?

Choosing what to grow

You can grow anything on your allotment that the climate and the site rules allow. This is, usually, primarily vegetables, with some fruit and flowers. The benefit of an allotment is that you have space to let your imagination run riot and to grow things that you don't have room for in your garden.

See *Grow Vegetables* and *Grow Fruit* in the *Green Essentials* series for details of the vegetables and fruit that you could grow.

If time and energy are not limited and you can visit the plot several times a week to tend and harvest, you can grow almost anything. But do be realistic. Nothing is more depressing than attempting too much and not really being successful with anything. If you know that time is limited, or you are just starting out, it is best to start with a simple range of crops that are relatively easy to grow, and don't need much attention.

It also makes sense not plant up the whole allotment to start with if you're not sure that you can cope with it.

Soil pests and diseases

One major factor limiting what you can grow may be the presence of persistent pests and diseases in the soil of your plot.

Because allotments have usually been grown on for decades, and not always treated well, certain pests and diseases can build up in the soil. Some can last for 20 years or more, even if the allotment is not used.

Don't let this put you off taking over a plot. Generally, using organic techniques to improve the soil will help to reduce the effects of soil borne pests and diseases – but cannot eliminate them. If onion white rot disease is present across the plot for example you may not be able to grow onions and garlic.

Generally, using organic techniques will help to reduce the effects of pests and diseases.

Persistent **soil problems**

Clubroot – a disease of cabbage family plants. On an infected plot, winter crops such as kale and sprouting broccoli are the best to try.

Whiterot – a disease of onions, garlic and leeks. If the soil is very badly infected you may not be able to grow garlic at all and onions may crop but only poorly. Leeks will usually survive.

Potato eelworm – a microscopic pest of potatoes that can reduce plant growth and cropping dramatically. Grow eelworm resistant varieties.

Crop rotation for healthy plants

Pests and diseases can build up in the soil if you grow plants of the same family in the same place year after year. To avoid this, divide the allotment into 4, equal sized, veg growing areas. Group plants of the same family together, and move them on each year to a new area, returning to the original plot in the 4th year. This is known as crop rotation. Where a problem such as clubroot or whiterot is severe, use a longer rotation.

A sample rotation plan

Area 1 – [peas and beans]; [beetroot and leaf beet]

Area 2 – [potatoes and tomatoes]

Area 3 – [onions, garlic and leeks]; [carrots and parsnips]

Area 4 – [cabbage family]; [courgettes and pumpkins]

[Vegetables in brackets] = plants in the same family
For more information see *Grow Vegetables* in the *Green Essentials* series.

Allotment vegetables – where **time is limited**

If time and/or energy is limited for running your allotment, grow crops that don't need too much regular attention. Here are some suggestions:

Onions and garlic Plant sets in spring or autumn. Must be kept weed free. No need for watering. Harvest early to late summer. Whole crop can be harvested at once. Store well for use through the winter.

Leeks Transplant young plants in June or July. May need weeding once or twice and watering occasionally if summer is dry. Will stand well over winter to be harvested as required. Leek roots helps to break up soil.

Broad beans Sow seed autumn or early spring. Little weeding required. Can be harvested all in one go. Freeze well.

Pumpkin and squash Transplant in early June (early summer). Mulch soil between plants with cardboard for weed control (and ground clearance). Harvest early autumn. No need to water once plants established. Store well for use through the winter.

Potatoes Can be planted in ground that is still quite weedy if necessary. Earth up once or twice to control weeds. Good crop to clear the land. Can also be grown under a mulch. Whole crop can be harvested at once.

Spinach beet and chard One sowing will crop for at least 6 months with little attention. Sow direct or transplant.

Beans for drying Use a variety of dwarf french bean sold for drying. Sow seed in early summer (starting under a cloche in colder areas). Weed once or twice. Harvest beans when pods are dry in autumn. A good storable source of protein.

Rainbow Chard. One sowing of this nutritious crop can provide fresh veg for six months.

Courgettes need to be picked every 2-3 days or you will soon have marrows instead!

Easy crops that need regular harvesting

Sweet corn Transplant in June. Watering not essential once established. Pick cobs when tassels are brown; eat fresh from the plant for maximum delight.

Courgettes Transplant in June. Pick every 2 or 3 days to avoid just getting marrows. May need to be watered in very dry weather.

Tomatoes Easy to grow outdoors in warmer areas, unless tomato blight disease strikes. Plant out in June. Pick fruits as they ripen.

Runner beans Grow up wigwam of canes. Transplant late May or sow direct in June. Pick beans regularly. Water in dry weather to maintain cropping.

Climbing french beans More reliable than runner beans in dry seasons.

The **cabbage** family

The cabbage family contains more traditional British vegetables than any other plant family. Many, particularly cabbage, broccoli, brussels sprouts and kale are easy to grow. The downside is that they are all prone to a wide range of pests and diseases which may be common on an allotment site. These include cabbage white caterpillars, mealy aphids, flea beetle, pigeons, cabbage rootfly and clubroot. Most are easy enough to prevent or treat if you are aware of them.

For more detailed information about growing individual vegetable crops, See *Grow Vegetables* in the *Green Essentials* series.

The cabbage family – attractive to pests and parents – not so popular with children.

Fruit

Your allotment may already have fruit trees or bushes on it – of varying age and states of health. If you don't intend to plant any new fruit in the short term, leave the existing plants in place, and monitor health and production over the next season.

Large **fruit trees** have value for wildlife and shade, so are worth keeping even if they don't fruit well. It's probably wise to take out small trees and fruit bushes and canes that are badly diseased – particularly if you are going to plant more of the same fruits.

Soft fruit – blackcurrants, gooseberries, redcurrants, raspberries and blackberries – are all good allotment candidates. They are easy enough to

grow, and give a good return from a bush or two within two years.
They don't require much attention, apart from the picking. Generally some protection against birds is needed - in the form of a proper netting walk-in cage, or simply nets draped over supports when the fruit is ripening.

Many allotment sites will not allow you to plant fruit trees, such as apples or plums, while others will approve as long as they are grown on a 'dwarfing rootstock' which means the trees will not grow too large.

For more information about growing fruit, see *Grow Fruit*, in the *Green Essentials* series.

Contrary to popular prejudice gooseberries can be delicious – and they're easy to grow.

Flowers for cutting and pest control

Flowers really brighten up an allotment. There are lots of easy to grow annuals that will provide colour over a long season. Many of these will self seed, so you only have to sow them once.

You can also grow your own pesticide-free cut flowers to brighten your home. Flowers also attract birds, bees and butterflies, and useful pest eating creatures such as hoverflies and lacewings. Grow these in and around the vegetable beds.

A selection of **easy to grow flowers**

ha = hardy annual

hp = hardy perennial

hhp = half hardy perennial

pc = attracts pest controlling insects

bb = attracts bees

cf = good as a cut flower

Bishop's flower *Ammi majus* **ha; pc; cf**

Dahlias hhp;cf

Egg-leaf spurge *Euphorbia oblongata* **hp** (short lived); **cf**

Cornflower *Centuarea cyanus* **ha; pc; bb; cf,**

Larkspur *Consolida ajacis* **ha; bb; cf**

Sunflowers *Helianthus annuus* **ha; pc; bb; cf**

Love in a mist *Nigella damascena and N hispanica* **ha;pc;bb; cf**

Pincushion flower *(Scabiosa atropurpurea)* **hp** (short lived); **bb; cf**

Pot marigold *Calendula officinalis* **ha; pc; cf**

Phacelia *Phacelia tancetifolia* **ha; pc; bb**

Fennel *Foeniculum vulgare* **hp; pc**

Candytuft *Iberis umbellata* **ha; pc; bb**

Californian poppy *Eschscholtzia californica* **ha; pc**

Goldenrod *Solidago virgaurea* **hp; pc; bb**

Time saving allotment tips

- Grow closely planted crops on narrow beds so they smother out weeds

- Use weed control mulches between widely spaced crops

- Cover unused areas with black plastic to stop weeds growing

- Don't water plants once they are established unless soil is very dry; yields may not be as high but you'll still get a crop and save a lot of time

- Make friends who will harvest crops for you while you are away

- Grow crops that don't need a lot of attention

- Keep a note of what you grew where – it saves time for next year's planning

- Select sowing times so veg doesn't all crop while you are on holiday

- Don't grow things that you don't like to eat

- Sow a green manure rather than leaving soil bare for months. This will improve the soil while preventing weeds from taking over

5

Keeping it going

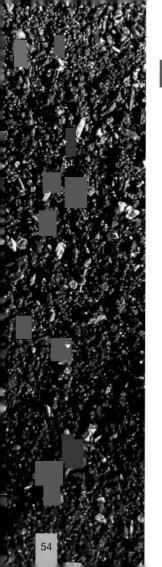

A healthy soil is the key

The key to successful allotment growing is a good fertile soil. Plants will then grow happily with little or no need for extra feeding or watering and will be more able to resist pest and disease attack.

You may be lucky enough to take on a well managed plot, in which case you will want to keep the soil in good condition. If you inherit a poor soil, then you will need to improve it over a period of years.

Whichever is the case, the techniques and materials are the same.

- Add bulky materials such as well rotted strawy manures, compost and leafmould. Spread as a surface mulch or dig into the top 20cm of soil.

- Don't work the soil when it is wet and sticky, or very dry.

- Don't rotavate every year, or dig unless it is really necessary.

- Protect the soil over winter with mulches and green manures.

Soil **improvers**

Manure – strawy cow or horse manure. Local farmers may deliver. Your allotment society should have details. If not from an organic source (or not well rotted) stack it under a sheet of polythene for 3-6 months.

Benefits – feeds plants and retains water.

Apply in spring and early summer to potato plot; also, if really well rotted, to pumpkins and cabbage family. Use 1-2 barrowloads per 10sq m.

Garden compost – make your own from all the weeds and crop wastes on your plot. Can also be bought in bags.

Benefits – feeds plants and retains water; also helps plants resist pest and disease.

Apply in spring and summer to all areas. Use 1-2 barrowloads per 10 sq m.

See *Create Compost* in the *Green Essentials* series for more information on making compost.

Local farmers may deliver manure in bulk direct to your allotment – your allotment society should be able to provide details.

Greenwaste compost – made on large scale composting sites. Can be bought in bags; in some areas it is available cheaply, in bulk.

Benefits – feeds plants and retains water. Slow release nitrogen; good source of potassium and phosphate. also helps plants resist pest and disease.

Apply at any time to any area.

Leafmould – make your own from autumn leaves. Some local councils will deliver leaves in the autumn.

Benefits – mainly water holding; low levels of plant foods.

Apply at any time to any areas. Freshly fallen leaves can be used to mulch plots over winter. After leaving them to rot for a year or two, they can also be dug into the soil.

Leaves take time to rot down – store in plastic bags to accelerate the decaying process or use them as they are as a covering mulch.

Mushroom compost – check local directories for suppliers; also some gardening catalogues. If not from an organic source, store it for a few months before use.

Benefits – feeds plants and retains water. Also tends to make the soil more alkaline.

Apply in spring and summer to cabbage family plot. Don't use on potatoes as it contains chalk which will raise the alkalinity.

Straw and hay – from farms and stables. 'Spoiled' bales may be cheaper and are equally good.

Benefits – weed suppressing mulch; water holding; some plant foods once broken down.

Apply as a mulch to any area once the soil has warmed up. Put sheets of cardboard underneath for improved weed control.

Local materials – you may find other suitable materials locally – such as spent hops from a brewery.

Check your local directories for suppliers of mushroom compost.

Grow your own soil improvers

A green manure is a crop that you grow to improve the soil and protect it from the elements.

Green manures are easiest to grow on an allotment over winter – sown in late summer and dug in the following spring. Green manures for winter use include grazing rye and winter tares. Crimson clover and phacelia will also stand the winter in many areas.

Buckwheat, mustard and fenugreek are green manures for spring and summer sowing on areas that will not otherwise be used for a couple of months or more. Always dig the plants in before they flower.

How to use a green manure to protect soil overwinter:

1. Sow the seed in late summer. As they grow, the plants use up available plant foods that would otherwise be washed out by the winter rains.

2. Next spring, chop up the green manure plants with a sharp spade and dig the chopped foliage into the ground.

3. Wait 2-3 weeks before sowing or planting.

Grazing rye – great for soil structure. Sow early to late autumn. Don't sow small seeded crops such as carrots and parsnips immediately after digging in grazing rye as germination may be inhibited for a few months.

Winter tares – a member of the legume family, this provides lots of nitrogen when dug in; good to grow overwinter before leafy crops such as cabbages. Sow in late summer.

Green manures. Phacelia tanacetifolia and crimson clover (inset) – dig plants in before they flower. You may also like to leave a patch to flower. The flowers are beautiful, and bees love them too.

Tips for keeping plants healthy

- Choose varieties with natural resistance

- Use compost and other soil improvers to keep soil full of vitality

- Use netting, horticultural fleece and other barriers to protect crops

- Check plants regularly; pick off pests and diseased material

- Make sure you know a friend from an enemy when checking for pests

- Use biological control such a 'nemaslug' for slugs where they are a real problem

- Use a crop rotation for vegetables to help stop the build-up of pests and diseases

- Plant flowers to attract hoverflies, lacewings and other creatures that eat pests – no need for pesticides

- Remove dead and dying plant material, and plants that have finished cropping. Put them on the compost heap to recycle the goodness they contain

who, what, where, when and why organic?

for all the answers and tempting offers go to www.whyorganic.org

- Mouthwatering offers on organic produce
- Organic places to shop and stay across the UK
- Seasonal recipes from celebrity chefs
- Expert advice on your food and health
- Soil Association food club – join for just £1 a month

Soil Association
the heart of organic food & farming

Resources

HDRA the organic organisation promoting organic gardening farming and food
www.hdra.org.uk
024 7630 3517

Soil Association the heart of organic food and farming
www.soilassociation.org
0117 929 0661

Allotments Regeneration Initiative
Tel: 0117 9631 551
ari@farmgarden.org.uk

National Society for Allotments and Leisure Gardeners
01536 266576
natsoc@nsalg.org.uk

The HDRA Encyclopedia of Organic Gardening
Dorling Kindersley
editor Pauline Pears

MAIL ORDER:

The Organic Gardening Catalogue
Organic seeds, composts, raised beds, barriers, traps and other organic gardening sundries. All purchases help to fund the HDRA's charity work.
www.organiccatalogue.com
0845 1301304

Green Gardener - composting
www.greengardener.co.uk
01394 420087

Suffolk Herbs – organic vegetable and herb seeds
www.suffolkherbs.com
01376 572456

Tamar Organics – organic seeds, composting
www.tamarorganics.co.uk 01822 834887

The Wormcast Company – organic fertiliser
www.thewormcastcompany.com
0845 605 5000

Want more organic gardening help?

Then join HDRA, the national charity
for organic gardening, farming and food.

As a member of HDRA you'll gain-
- free access to our Gardening Advisory Service
- access to our three gardens in Warwickshire, Kent
  and Essex and to 10 more gardens around the UK
- opportunities to attend courses and talks or visit
  other gardens on Organic Gardens Open Weekends
- discounts when ordering from the Organic
  Gardening Catalogue
- discounted membership of the Heritage
  Seed Library
- quarterly magazines full of useful information

You'll also be supporting-
- the conservation of heritage seeds
- an overseas organic advisory service to help
  small-scale farmers in the tropics
- Duchy Originals HDRA Organic Gardens for Schools
- HDRA Organic Food For All campaign
- research into organic agriculture

To join HDRA ring: **024 7630 3517**
email: **enquiries@hdra.org.uk**
or visit our website: **www.hdra.org.uk**

Charity No. 298104

HDRA
the organic
organisation